Cover: bow of *No Logic*, Swan 112. (C Borlenghi)
Page 1: cruising, 1920. (Rosenfeld Collection)
Pages 2 and 3: yachts of the late nineteenth and early twentieth century. (Studio Faggioni)
Previous pages: *Ingomar* – schooner, 1903. (Rosenfeld Collection)

SAIL

A PHOTOGRAPHIC
CELEBRATION OF
SAIL POWER

SAIL

A PHOTOGRAPHIC CELEBRATION OF SAIL POWER

ADLARD COLES NAUTICAL
LONDON

Published by Adlard Coles Nautical
An imprint of A&C Black Publishers Ltd
36 Soho Square, London, W1D 3QY
www.adlardcoles.com

Copyright © 2005, 2010 Mondadori Electa S.p.A.
English translation © 2006 Mondadori Electa S.p.A.

Originally published by Mondadori Electa S.p.A. in 2005
First English Language edition published by Adlard Coles Nautical in 2006
Published in paperback by Adlard Coles Nautical in 2010

ISBN: 978-1-4081-2995-1

PHOTOGRAPHIC CREDITS:
Beken of Cowes
Carlo Borlenghi/SeaSee.it
Guido Cantini/SeaSee.it
Vincent Curutchet/Dppi/SeaSee.it
Steve Emby/SeaSee.it
Francesco Ferri/SeaSee.it
Daniel Forster/Dppi/SeaSee.it
Andrea Francolini/Dppi/SeaSee.it
Beppe Franzoni
Lucio Gelsi
The Edwin Levick Collection, Mystic Seaport Museum
Jean-Marie Liot/Dppi/SeaSee.it
Giles Martin-Raget/SeaSee.it
Thierry Martinez/SeaSee.it
Franco Pace
Simon Palfrader
Lino Pastorelli
The Rosenfeld Collection, Mystic Seaport Museum
Cory Silken
James Robinson Taylor/SeaSee.it
Henri Thibault/Dppi/SeaSee.it
Rick Tomlinson
Paul Todd/Dppi/SeaSee.it
Tim Wright

EDITED BY:
Fabio Ratti

GRAPHIC DESIGN AND ART DIRECTION:
Claudia Bonfanti

EDITING:
Alberto Santangelo

ENGLISH TRANSLATION:
Lois Tutel

ENGLISH-LANGUAGE TYPESETTING:
Michael Shaw

PRINTED AND BOUND IN CHINA BY C&C OFFSET PRINTING CO

ACKNOWLEDGEMENTS
For their invaluable help with photographic research:
Gruppo Ermenegildo Zegna – Nautor Group
Rolex – Southern Wind Shipyard – Wally Yacht.

Page 8: *Adela* – schooner from 1903, rebuilt in 1995. (C Borlenghi)
Previous pages: *Kauris II* – Maxi Yacht Club, Emerald Coast, 1999. (C Borlenghi)
Opposite page: *Il Moro di Venezia* – America's Cup, San Diego, 1992. (C Borlenghi)

'I'LL DO BUSINESS WITH ANYONE,
BUT I'LL ONLY GO SAILING WITH GENTLEMEN.'

THE PHRASE ABOVE IS ATTRIBUTABLE TO JP MORGAN, WEALTHY BANKER AND CELEBRATED SHIPOWNER OF THE 1930S. AT THE TIME, SAILING WAS IN ITS GOLDEN AGE AND THE PHRASE IS NOW INSTRUCTIONAL: SAILING, AS MORGAN MAKES CLEAR, WAS FIRST AND FOREMOST A GENTLEMEN'S AFFAIR, ITS PRACTITIONERS MEN OF UNLIMITED FINANCES AND WITH FAMILY HISTORIES DATING BACK CENTURIES. TELLINGLY, WHEN THE SELF-MADE MAN, MERCHANT AND YACHTSMAN THOMAS LIPTON SPENT A FORTUNE BRINGING THE AMERICA'S CUP TO ENGLAND IN 1899, THE MEMBERS OF THE ROYAL YACHT SQUADRON OF COWES MADE THEIR DISDAIN CLEAR BY CALLING HIM A GROCER. THANKFULLY, THIS TYPE OF SAILING IS NO LONGER WITH US. TODAY, SAILING TAKES MANY FORMS, AND ADDRESSES A VARIETY OF TASTES AND BUDGETS, FROM THE OCEAN-GOING TO THE HISTORICAL, TO SINGLE AND MULTIHULL CHALLENGES, REGATTAS AND CRUISES. YET, SOMETHING OF AN INHERITANCE REMAINS FROM THE YACHTSMEN OF THE EARLY PART OF THE LAST CENTURY. MORE SAILING ENTHUSIASTS THAN EVER ARE CHOOSING TO BUILD AND REBUILD WOODEN BOATS WHICH ARE ALMOST CERTAINLY SLOWER, LESS COMFORTABLE AND MORE COSTLY THAN THEIR CONTEMPORARY EQUIVALENTS. CLEAR EVIDENCE THAT J P MORGAN'S DICTUM IS STILL RELEVANT.

THIS BOOK IS A PHOTOGRAPHIC JOURNEY BETWEEN THE GOLDEN AGE OF SAILING AND MODERN AND CONTEMPORARY YACHTING. IT IS AN ALBUM FORMED OF IMAGES CAPTURED BY THE WORLD'S MOST ACCOMPLISHED NAUTICAL PHOTOGRAPHERS. STANLEY ROSENFELD (US) AND BEKEN OF COWES (UK) WERE THE FIRST TO IMMORTALISE THE AGE OF THE GREAT SCHOONERS, THE HERALDED CHALLENGES BETWEEN THE BIG BOATS, THE J CLASS AND OTHER NOTABLE DESIGN CLASSICS FROM THE BEGINNING OF THE LAST CENTURY. THIS PERIOD WAS DOMINATED BY THE AMERICANS AND THE BRITISH, WITH THE LATTER FAVOURING CUTTERS THAT WERE NARROW AND HEAVY AND THE FORMER OPTING FOR CUTTERS THAT WERE WIDE AND LIGHT, WITH VERY LITTLE DRAFT.

THESE DIFFERENCES, SO EVIDENT IN THE FIRST CHALLENGES OF THE AMERICA'S CUP, DISAPPEARED IN PART THANKS TO THE ONSET OF MORE SOPHISTICATED EXCHANGES OF INFORMATION AND TECHNOLOGIES, BUT PRINCIPALLY SO THAT BEST ADVANTAGE COULD BE TAKEN OF THE PARAMETERS AND TONNAGE RULES GOVERNING THE VARIOUS HANDICAP SYSTEMS THAT FOLLOWED OVER THE COURSE OF TIME.

ROSENFELD'S AND BEKEN'S PIONEERING ACTION PHOTOGRAPHY AT SEA FRAMES ON END OF THE TRANSITION FROM IMPECCABLY-DRESSED SKIPPERS AT THE WHEEL SPORTING SOCIAL BLAZER AND TIE, TO THE HULLS MADE OF CARBON AND SAILS CONSTRUCTED OF KEVLAR SUCH AS WE NOW REGULARLY EXPECT OF OUR YACHTS. (NOT TO MENTION THE MULTIHULLS WHICH CONTINUE TO BETTER BOTH SPEED RECORDS AND THE AMOUNT OF ADVERTISABLE SURFACE AREA FOR THEIR SPONSOR'S LOGOS.) THEIR ENDURING LEGACY IS FELT THROUGHOUT THIS BOOK.

Steel frames are fixed to a wooden stem in a service yard at the beginning of the last century. (Yachting Library Archive)

Waterwitch, an English schooner designed in 1880 by Camper and Nicholson. Right: a two masted schooner with auric sails set to shore.

'A very handsome cutter ... designer by Mr G L Watson for the Duke of Abruzzi ...' Thus the English press welcomed the *Bona* in 1897. (Yachting Library Archive)

King George V and his *Brittania*, designed by Watson, sunk in the English Channel in 1936 with a load of explosives, as willed in the testament of its very jealous owner. (Yachting Library Archive)

Sailing during the 1905 Kaiser's Cup (by order of the Emperor of Germany). Shown here are 11 hulls ready at the start line of the 3,000 nautical mile journey from New York to The Lizard on the south west coast of England. (Rosenfeld Collection)

Two images that illustrate the enormous sail area of yachts during the early years of the last century.
(Rosenfeld Collection)
(Yachting Library Archive)

Pen Duick, a project of William Fife, and a family boat of Eric Tabarlys', arguably the greatest sailor of our time.
(Studio Faggioni)   (G M Raget)

The five great yachts collectively known as 'The Big Five', from the left: *Lulworth*, *Shamrock IV*, *Westward*, *Brittania*, *White Heather II*. (Beken of Cowes)

The hull of *Lulworth* during the first phase of its restoration in the shipyard at Viareggio. Twenty-five percent of the original steel was used. (L Gelsi)

 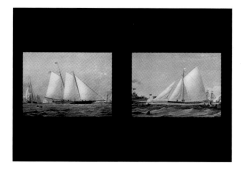 

America was a schooner with a length of 108ft (33m) and width of 24ft (7m). Sporting a solid wooden hull made from oak, she had four master cabins and accommodation for a crew of 15. (Studio Faggioni)

Two distinct design philosophies; *America*, left, and *Voltant*, a 48 ton English cutter. (Yachting Library Archive)

Four Classic English cutters from the end of the nineteenth century characterised by straight bows and the thrust of their pronounced sterns. (Yachting Library Archive)

Atlantic, a schooner designed in 1903 by William Gardener of Boston. The design of the *Star*, the celebrated Olympic class, is also his. (Rosenfeld Collection)

Adela, launched in 1903, is a classic schooner of the 230 ton period. She was restored using modern materials (carbon) and technology (winches on deck).

The New York 50 is one of many monohull classes designed at the start of the last century by Nat Herreshoff for members of the New York Yacht Club. (Rosenfeld Collection)

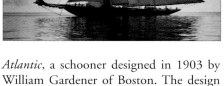   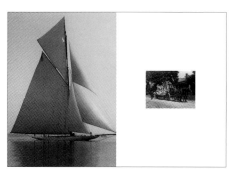

Reliance, defender of the America's cup of 1903, represents the most advanced evolution of the racing yacht. Its waterline length was 94ft (29m) but measured 153ft (47m) when out of the water.

Reliance had 30 or so crew members in addition to the afterguard, the so-called 'mind' of the boat, who dressed in dark colours to distinguish themselves from the ordinary crewmembers who dressed in white. (Rosenfeld Collection)

A ruling in 1903 brought about hulls with long bows, thereby instituting a difference in a vessel's waterline length when upright and when heeled over on its beam. Right, a 'tender' of the period takes sails to dry. (Yachting Library Archive)

(Herreshoff Museum)

The skeletal frame of *Lulworth* ready to receive planking, deck and fittings. In a ten year period (1920-1930), it entered 200 regattas, winning 47 times and placing 11. (L Gelsi)

Two beautiful, American schooners, both relatively small for the period, measuring slightly more than 60ft (18m) each in length. (Rosenfeld Collection)

Vim, of 1938, was the best 12 Metre S I of its time. Left: two boats of the same class, which from 1958 onwards began to compete in the America's Cup. (Yachting Library Archive)

Right: *Terrenia II*, a 15 Metre International Class. Designed by Frederick Shepherd in 1913, it was launched the following year as *Sappho II*. (L Pastorelli)

Tirrenia II, under sail. Right: *Linnet* a New York 30 designed by Herreshoff. The class enjoyed great success during the period. (L Pastorelli)

Sailing during the Argentario Regatta which, each year, attracts the best of the international fleet of period boats to one of the most beautiful Italian regatta settings. (L Pastorelli)

North American fishermen were so competitive among themselves that they organised an international competition that lasted 20 years. The photograph above is from the 1938 edition of the International Fisherman's Races. The two schooners engaged are the *Gertrude L. Thebaud* (US) and *Bluenose* (Canada), holder of the title since 1921. (Rosenfeld Collection)

THE CRADLE OF YACHTING

DESPITE THE FACT THAT THE EXACT DATE OF THE BIRTH OF YACHTING AS A NAUTICAL PASTIME IS DISPUTED (THE DUTCH AND RUSSIANS BOTH LAY CLAIM TO THE TITLE), THERE IS EVIDENCE TYING IT TO THE FOUNDING OF THE FIRST YACHT CLUBS. ONE OF THE FIRST DOCUMENTED OF THESE, THE WATER CLUB IN CORK, IRELAND, KNOWN SUBSEQUENTLY AS THE ROYAL CORK YACHT CLUB, IS ALSO NOTABLE FOR ITS LONGEVITY, FOUNDED IN 1720, THE 'WATER' STILL EXISTS TO THIS DAY.

IN THE UNITED STATES, THE ORIGINS OF YACHTING (AS AN OCCUPATION) DATE BACK TO THE END OF THE SEVENTEENTH CENTURY, A DIRECT RESULT OF THE DUTCH COLONISTS WHO ESTABLISHED THEMSELVES IN NEW YORK AFTER THE ENGLISH CONQUEST OF 1664. YACHTING AS A LEISURE PURSUIT SUCH AS WE UNDERSTAND IT TODAY, HOWEVER, ONLY DEVELOPED TOWARDS THE END OF THE NINETEENTH CENTURY. MUCH, IT SHOULD BE NOTED, IS OWED TO JOHN COX STEVENS WHO, ASIDE FROM FOUNDING THE NEW YORK YACHT CLUB IN 1884, OWNED THE SCHOONER AMERICA, WHICH WENT ON TO WIN THE ONE HUNDRED GUINEAS CUP – THE CURRENT-DAY AMERICA'S CUP – IN ENGLISH WATERS IN 1851. IT WAS, BY ALL ACCOUNTS, A DECISIVE YEAR FOR AMERICAN YACHTING. IN ADDITION TO RIDDING ITSELF OF THE PERSISTENT IRONIC CONDESCENSION BY THE ENGLISH, AMERICAN CLIPPERS OUTPACES ENGLISH HULLS ALL ALONG THE ESTABLISHED COMMERCIAL ROUTES, BRITISH YACHTSMEN EVIDENTLY BELIEVING THAT THE OPEN OCEAN WAS NO PLACE TO PRACTICE SUCH A HIGHLY REFINED SPORT AS SAILING.

THE SPORT OF SAILING, PROPELLED ALONG, AS IT WAS, THANKS TO THE NECESSITIES OF COMMERCE, WAS GIVEN A SIGNIFICANT BOOST BY THE STRONG MARITIME INSTINCTS OF THE ENGLISH ARISTOCRACY. IN 1815, LORD GRANTHAM AND A GROUP OF NOBLEMEN FOUNDED THE YACHT CLUB, THE SIMPLICITY OF ITS NAME BEING SYMPTOMATIC OF ITS FOUNDING FATHERS' MODEST AMBITIONS. TWO YEARS LATER, THE RULING PRINCE REGENT GEORGE AUGUSTUS FREDERICK BECAME A MEMBER. THEN IN 1820, HAVING ASCENDED TO THE THRONE AS GEORGE IV, THE TITLE OF 'ROYAL' WAS BESTOWED ON THE CLUB, WITH THE RESULT THAT THE CROWN CONSEQUENTLY ACQUIRED ENORMOUS INFLUENCE OVER ALL NAUTICAL MATTERS THEREAFTER. THE EXTENT OF THIS INFLUENCE CAN BE SEEN IN THE FOLLOWING PRIVILEGE ACCORDED TO THE CLUB IN 1830 BY GEORGE IV'S SUCCESSOR, HIS YOUNGER BROTHER WILLIAM IV: '[THIS PRIVILEGE IS BESTOWED] AS A SIGN OF GRACIOUS APPROVAL FOR THE GREAT, NATIONAL USE OF THIS INSTITUTION, EMBELLISHING ITSELF WITH THE NAME OF THE ROYAL YACHT SQUADRON OF WHICH HIS MAJESTY DOES GRACIOUSLY DEIGN HIMSELF AS ITS RULER'.

THE SPREAD OF THE YACHT CLUB AS AN IMPORTANT NAUTICAL INSTITUTION CONTINUED DURING THE VICTORIAN ERA, WITH NEW REGATTAS SPRINGING UP IN COWES AND THE EXCITING DEVELOPMENT OF THE BIG BOAT CHALLENGES. THE SO-CALLED GOLDEN AGE OF SAILING HAD ARRIVED.

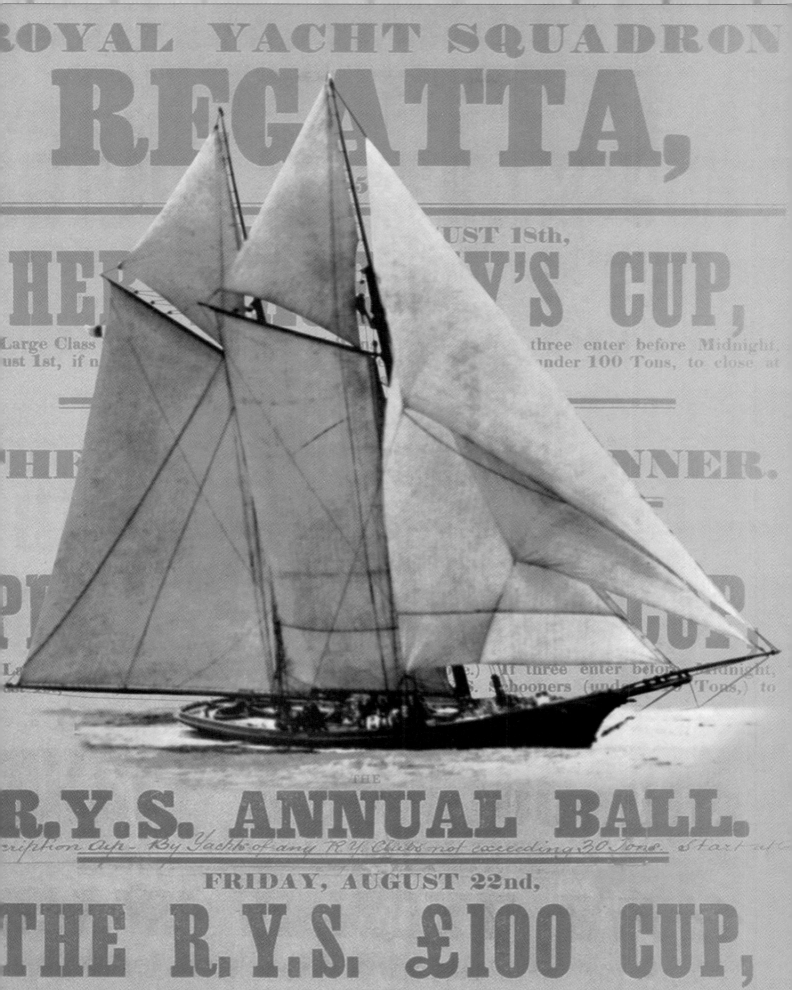

Two yachts at Les Volles di Saint Tropez, an event held in October on the Cote d'Azur, closing the cycle of period regattas on the Mediterranean. (C Borlenghi)

A modern design from Hinckley (right), the distinguished American yard, has little to envy in terms of equalling the elegance of the cruising yacht of the 1940s, shown left. (L Pastorelli)

A forest of wooden masts in Porto Santo Stefano during the annual gathering of period boats at the Argentario. (L Pastorelli)

Two contrasting sailing concepts: left, a modern cruiser/racer; right, a very modern Spirit of Tradition Class.
(G M Raget)   (C Borlenghi)

The Caribbean, a sailing paradise even when at anchor. (C Borlenghi)

Adela, shown here taking first place in the Spirit of Tradition Class at the Maxi Yacht Rolex Cup of 2005. (C Borlenghi)

Three bowmen at work. This is a key role at race starts, when clear instructions need to be given to the helmsman about buoys, etc. (S Palfrader)

Under gennaker in Portofino during the Zegna Trophy. The gennaker was first introduced in 1981. (C Borlenghi)

The Swan's typically narrow bowline counter-balances the boat's heeling. (C Borlenghi)

Rob Stephens, second from the top in the photograph, climbs the mizzen of *Ranger*. His specialisation was rigging, while his brother, Olin, designed the lines of the boat. (Levick Collection)

The replica of *Ranger*, the fastest of the J's built during the period, was created under the J Class rule, which was established in 2000 and formed the basis for building replicas using original plans. (C Silken)

Tom Sopwith, elegant in regulation blazer, at the wheel of *Endeavour*. The crew's coveralls are his invention, derived from the field of aeronautics. (Rosenfeld Collection)

The deck of the new *Ranger* shows a mix of classic and ultramodern elements. (C Silken)

Emilia was designed by Nat Herreshoff as a 12 Metre International Class but, prior to its launch, was converted into a schooner for cruising. (L Pastorelli)

Mariette, designed and launched by Nat Herreshoff in 1915, is at 104ft (32m), among the few large schooners still sailing. (L Pastorelli)

Adix, a splendid three masted schooner, is photographed off Saint Tropez. (C Borlenghi)

Stormy Weather, designed in 1933 by Olin Stephens.

A period schooner, perfectly maintained, expresses all its power at Antigua Classic Yacht Weeks, a celebrated event for lovers of period boats. (F Pace)

Magic Carpet, left, and *Whitefin*, designed in 1983 by Bruce Finn. (C Borlenghi)

Tuamata, a 77ft (23m) Wally Yacht, takes second in class at the Maxi Yacht Rolex Cup in 2002. Right: *Alexia* an 80ft (24m) Wally designed by Reichel/Pugh. (C Borlenghi)

Alexi won the Maxi Yacht Rolex Cup at Port Cervo in 2002, six years after its launch. It is now enjoying success as *Damiani our dream*. (C Borlenghi)

Launched in 1999, the Spirit of Tradition Class *Antonisa*, is a modern boat built along classic lines. The design is by Bruce King. (C Borlenghi)

Left: Maxis crossing during a regatta. Right: *Southern Star*, a maxi of the South African yard Southern Wind Shipyard. (C Borlenghi)

Sea, spray, sun and wind on the waters of the Emerald Coast. (C Borlenghi)

Yankee, designed by Frank Paine, was built for the America's Cup of 1930 by a Boston-based syndicate. It lost in the defender selection trials against *Enterprise*, not because the latter was the better choice, but, according to rumour, because a Boston defender was unacceptable to the New York Yacht Club. The only American J Class to race in English waters, *Yankee* was scrapped in 1941. (Rosenfeld Collection)

J Class

T HE J CLASS HOLDS A PARTICULAR FASCINATION FOR THE YACHTSMAN. THERE HAVE CERTAINLY BEEN LARGER AND FASTER YACHTS THROUGHOUT SAILING HISTORY, BUT NONE HAVE EQUALLED THE J'S ELEGANCE OR HER ABILITY TO INSPIRE. FROM THEIR UNIQUE DIMENSIONS, TO THEIR STAGGERINGLY HIGH CONSTRUCTION COSTS, THE CAPTIVATING AND MAJESTIC PHOTOGRAPHIC IMAGES THEY INSPIRED AT THE HANDS OF STANLEY ROSENFELD AND BEKEN OF COWES, THE J CLASS IS A BREED OF YACHT HISTORICALLY SYNONYMOUS WITH 'ARISTOCRACY', 'WEALTH' AND THAT COVER-ALL TERM, THE 'UPPER CLASS'.

HOWEVER, WITH THE ONSET OF THE SECOND WORLD WAR, INCREASINGLY PROHIBITIVE COSTS AND DWINDLING RESOURCES (NOT TO MENTION THE PRACTICAL IF NOT FORMAL DECLINE OF THE MONARCHY), CONSTRUCTION OF THE J CLASS CAME TO AN END. OF THE TEN BUILT, SIX WERE AMERICAN AND FOUR WERE BRITISH, AND ALL EXCEPT ONE (*VELSHEDA*, 1933) WERE BUILT WITH THE AMERICA'S CUP IN MIND. WITH THEIR SPECIFICATIONS FORMALLY DEFINED IN THE UNIVERSAL RULE, THE CORE CHARACTERISTICS OF THE J CLASS INCLUDED A WATERLINE LENGTH OF 76-87FT (23-27M), DISPLACEMENT OF APPROXIMATELY 160 TONS AND MAST HEIGHTS IN EXCESS OF 160FT (49M). THE J CLASS' SPANKER ALONE WEIGHED ONE TON, WHILE THE SPINNAKER MEASURED OVER 18,000 SQUARE FT (1670 SQ M). THE LARGE SCALE MEASUREMENTS WERE REFLECTED IN THE CONSTRUCTION COSTS, TOO. *ENTERPRISE*, DEFENDER OF THE 1930 AMERICA'S CUP, WAS BUILT FOR THE PRINCELY SUM OF ONE MILLION DOLLARS (ROUGHLY EIGHT MILLION POUNDS TODAY).

NINETEEN THIRTY-FOUR IS ARGUABLY THE YEAR IN WHICH POPULAR INTEREST IN THE J CLASS PEAKED. IN THE UK, IN PARTICULAR, SHIPOWNERS CLOSELY FOLLOWED THE FORTUNES OF *ENDEAVOUR* WITH ALL THE FEVERED INTEREST THAT BEFITS A LARGE PUBLIC SPECTACLE. NOT ONLY WERE WAGERS MADE, BUT IN ORDER TO SATISFY THE LARGE CROWDS WATCHING THE REGATTA FROM THE SHORELINE THE COMPETING YACHTS WERE RENDERED IMMEDIATELY DISTINGUISHABLE FROM AFAR THROUGH THE USE OF DIFFERENT COLOURED VARNISHES.

ONLY THREE JS REMAIN TODAY, ALL, INCIDENTALLY, BUILT IN ENGLAND: *ENDEAVOUR*, *VELSHEDA* AND *SHAMROCK V*. RESTORATION OF THESE HULLS REMAINS MUCH IN DISCUSSION, WITH THE BOATS UNDERGOING SUBSTANTIAL TRANSFORMATION NOT ONLY IN THEIR GENERAL ASPECT, BUT ALSO AS FAR AS MATERIALS AND OTHER FITTINGS ARE CONCERNED. THERE IS EVEN A REPLICA OF THE *RANGER* SAILING, AND OTHER PROJECTS UNDER WAY, SUGGESTING THAT THE J CLASS IS NOW ENJOYING A MOMENT OF RENEWED SPLENDOUR.

Tikertitan, a 90ft (27m) futuristic Wally Yacht that was launched in 1998. (C Borlenghi)

Black carbon sails reflect the light at Newport. (C Borlenghi)

Italia, part of the 12 metre International Class, is seen manoeuvring on Lake Como. (C Borlenghi)

Three appendages and a retractable bowsprit are now standard for a modern ocean-going maxi, shown here thanks to transparent waters at the Rolex Trophy Series in Australia. (A Francolini)

Amer Sports One during an around the world race.

Amer Sports Two, with its all female crew, is a particularly fast VO 60. The design is by Bruce Farr. (Nautor's Swan Archive)

Amer Sports One, whose skipper is Grant Dalton, is a VO 60, the class designed to compete in the Volvo Ocean Race around the world in real time. (Nautor's Swan Archive)

Amer Sports One during the fourth stage of the 2001-2002 race around the world in which the mythic Cape Horn is rounded twice.

Two images of the Nautor Challenge during a Volvo Ocean Race. The event is currently run in nine stages for a total of 32,700 miles

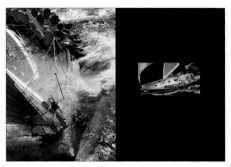

The Ermengildo Zegna Trophy, Spring Regattas, Portofina, 2005. (S Palfreder)

Launched under the name *Shockwave* in 2002 in New Zealand, *Alfa Romeo* is a 90ft (27m) maxi and is probably the fastest in its category. (C Borlenghi)

Right: *Cuor di Leone*; Left, *Lady in Red*, two Swan 68s which are always very competitive.

The most exclusive custom monohull in the world is probably the Swan 45, designed by German Frers and in production since 2002. (C Borlenghi)

An ocean wave successfully hides a Swan during a regatta. (R Wright)

A gennaker furl is shown on board *Viriella*, the maxi owned by Vittorio Moretti. (C Borlenghi)

My Song, a Nauta 75 belonging to Pierluigi Loropiana, is shown during a regatta at Portofino. (C Borlenghi)

Thirty thousand dollars (approximately seventeen thousand pounds) torn to shreds in an instant. (C Borlenghi)

On the genoa, the unmistakable mark of the sail loft North Sails, a maxi favourite. (C Borlenghi)

The VO 60 *Amer Sports One* nears Cape Town while hidden by an ocean wave. (C Borlenghi)

The Maxi Yacht Rolex Cup in Porto Cervo, a leading maxi event since the 1980's. (C Borlenghi)

Solleone, designer by German Frers and measuring 82ft (25m), is Nautor's jewel in the crown. (C Bolenghi)

The famous Antigua Sailing Week is a sailor's paradise. (Yachting Library Archive)

The Swan Regatta in 2005, which is run each year in Newport, Rhode Island in waters that have hosted hundreds of America's Cup regattas. (D Foster)

Sails constructed in 3DL, a patent controlled by North Sails, are widely used by the more competitive maxis. (B Franzoni)

Virtuelle is a hull design by Andrea Valicelli but with deck and interior by Philippe Starck. The French designer's touch is apparent throughout. (C Borlenghi)

MAXI YACHT

THE J CLASS OF THE 1930S OCCUPIED A PLACE IN THE YACHTING FIRMAMENT THAT HAS NOW BEEN TAKEN UP BY THE EQUALLY IMPOSING MAXI YACHT. WHILE THERE IS NO PRECISE DEFINITION OF THE MAXI WITH RESPECT TO DESIGN SPECIFICATIONS, IT CAN BE SAID THAT MAXIS ARE PREDOMINANTLY CUSTOM DESIGNED AND BUILT, HAVE MOVEABLE BALLASTS AND OSCILLATING KEELS, ARE DESIGNATED AS EITHER A RACER OR CRUISER (OR STRADDLE BOTH, RACER/CRUISER), AND GENERALLY ACT AS A TESTING GROUND FOR SAIL TRIM AND FITTINGS SOLUTIONS WHICH ARE OFTEN ADOPTED LATER ON FOR MASS PRODUCTION BOATS.

AS WITH THE J CLASS, MAXIS ALSO INVOKE, IF A LITTLE FALSELY, THE ROMANTIC FIGURE OF THE GENTLEMAN-SKIPPER IN POSSESSION NOT ONLY OF AN AMPLE WALLET AND SURROUNDED BY A CREW OF WIZENED SAILING PROFESSIONALS, BUT HONOUR-BOUND TO A SENSE OF THE PROPER RULES OF THE GAME. THE ENGLISHMAN TOM SOPWITH, FOR INSTANCE, OWNER OF THE 1937 LAUNCHED J CLASS *ENDEAVOUR II* (THAT WOULD LOSE TO *RANGER* IN THE VERY LAST AMERICA'S CUP TO USE THE J CLASS), DIDN'T HESITATE TO FIRE CREW MEMBERS WHOSE EGOS AND PAY PACKETS HE THOUGHT HAD GROWN TOO LARGE. (SOPWITH IS ALSO NOTED FOR HIS INSISTENCE ON MORE ELEGANT AND COMFORTABLE INTERIORS.) TODAY, SUCH CHICANERY, IT GOES WITHOUT SAYING, IS PAR FOR THE COURSE.

NONETHELESS, THE EXTENT TO WHICH THE MAXI YACHT CONCEPT IS NOW OPEN TO VARIED INTERPRETATION IS NICELY ILLUSTRATED IN THE FIGURE OF LUCA BASSINI, A WEALTHY ITALIAN YACHTSMAN FAMOUSLY ADDICTED TO CRUISING COMFORT BUT NOT WILLING TO SACRIFICE ANY RELATED PERFORMANCE. THE RESULT, WALLY YACHTS, IS BASSINI'S ANSWER TO A TRADITION THAT DEMANDS IN EQUAL PARTS FINE CRAFTSMANSHIP, SPEED, GRACE AND PERENNIAL COMPETITIVENESS IN THE WORLD'S MOST CHALLENGING SAILING COURSES FROM NEWPORT TO SARDINIA'S EMERALD COAST. PREDICTABLY, WHERE BASSINI AND OTHERS OF HIS ILK OFTEN STRUGGLE, IS IN FITTING THEIR SOMETIMES RADICAL DESIGNS WITHIN A LARGER FRAMEWORK OF HANDICAPS CAPABLE OF RESULTING IN CLASSIFICATION.

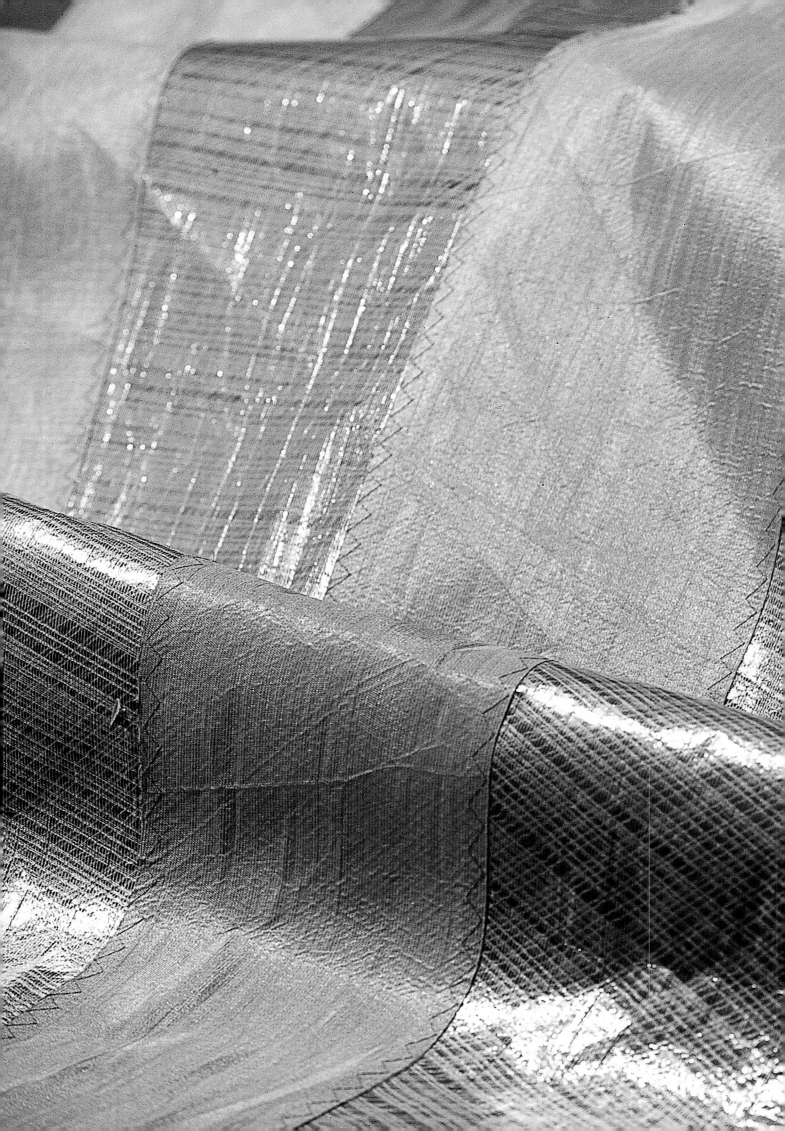

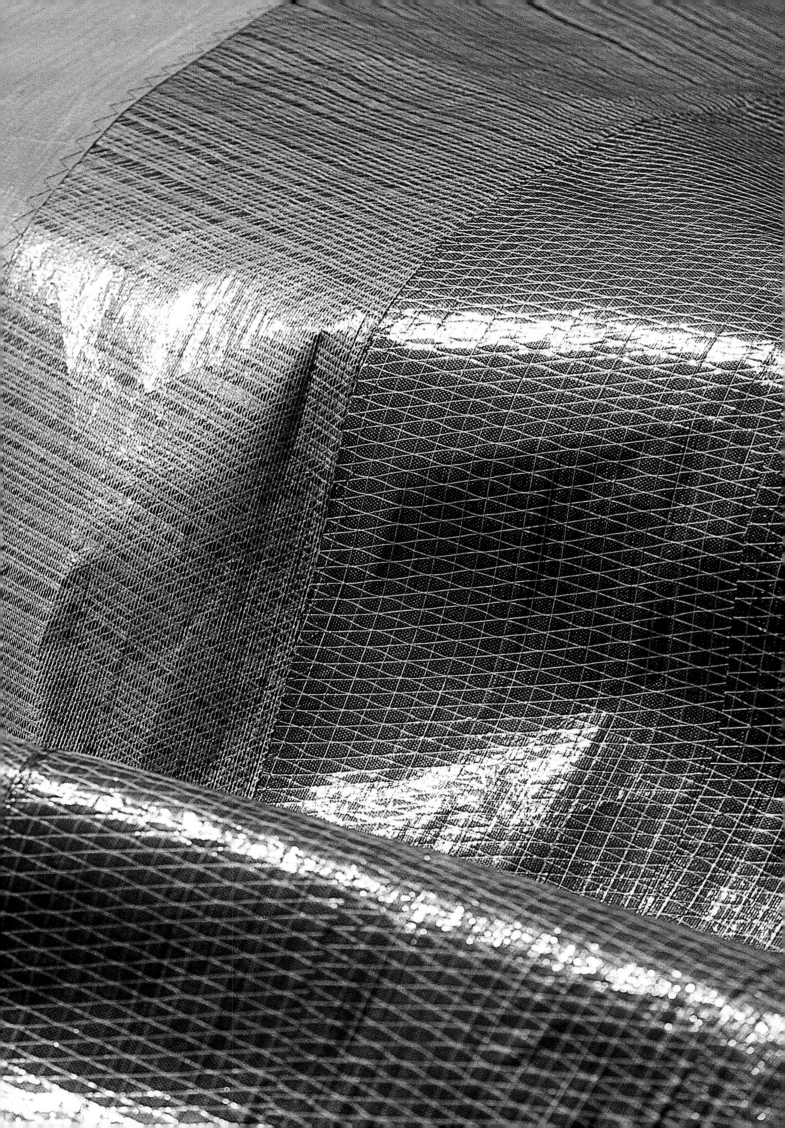

Konika Minolta (upwind), and *Skandia Wild Thing* are shown at the Rolex Trophy Series 2004 in Sydney. (A Francolini)

Ulisee, left, is a 105ft (32m) maxi designed by Frers for Patrizio Bertelli. Right: *Ulisee* in competition in the waters of Antigua.

Capri's Faraglioni (isolated rocks of the sea) during Three Gulfs Week. (C Borlenghi)

Wally *Tiketitoo* may look like a toy model in this photo but her 89ft (27m) length and 20ft (6m) width are the genuine article. (G M Raget)

The Swan 70 *Bugia Bianca* at the Swan Cup in Sardinia, September 2000. (G Cantini)

Zana, 98ft (30m) in length, is New Zealand's largest ocean-going maxi. This photo, taken during the Rolex Sydney-Hobart, shows the crew at the stern. (D Forster)

The Pirelli Regatta – Santa Margherita, Ligure, 2005. (C Borlenghi)

Zaca is shown competing during the Hahn Premium Race Week, Hamilton Island, Australia, 2004. (A Francolini)

Alexia, designed and built by Wally yachts. (C Borlenghi)

The bowman frees the track of the spinnaker during manoeuvres as Antigua Sailing Week 2005. (D Forster)

The crew of *All Smoke* are ready to recover the spinnaker of this Nauta 78 designed by Reichel/Pugh. This image was captured only moments after the photograph in the previous caption. (R Tomlinson)

Alfa Romeo is shown at Hamilton Race Week in 2005. HRW is a prestigious invitational event organised by the Royal Bermuda Yacht Club. (A Francolini)

The Rolex Antigua Sailing Week is considered to be among the top five most important regattas in the world, attracting on average over 200 boats annually. (D Forster)

Built to be the fastest monohull in the world, *Mari Cha* is 138ft (42m) in length but weighs a meagre 50 tons. Only the minimum indispensable items are kept below deck. (D Forster)

Mari Cha's 33ft (10m) width is in evidence in this shot. (T Martinez)

Unfurled, a 34 metre yacht designed by Frers, is a maxi that competes in the 'cruising division'. (C Borlenghi)

Morning Glory is a Maxi 80 designed by Reichel/Pugh and built with the most advanced methods and materials. (D Forster)

Rolex is the sponsor of many of the most important race events in the world. (D Forster)

Charis, an Italian maxi in the waters of Portofino during the Zegna Trophy. (C Borlenghi)

Monohulls are shown nearing buoy markers. (C Borlenghi)

Melges 24 during the Semaine Nautique Internationale de la Mediterrannee, Marseille, 2005. (C Borlenghi)

Joe Fly, a Melges 24, during the 2005 Italian Class Championship in Portisco. (J R Taylor)

Two images that demonstrate the tiny performance differentials that separate most monohull classes.
(A Francolini)   (J M Liot)

Farr 40 in competition. Similar hull types often make for highly spectacular race events. (Yachting Library Archive)

The 66ft (20m) *AAPT* took fourth in the 2004 Sydney-Hobart. The event, which dates back to 1945, is 630 miles of extremely taxing racing that finishes in the Roaring Forties. (D Forster)

THE GREAT REGATTAS

I October 1661. A parade of boats slowly advances down the Thames, the wind against them. In front, two yachts fly royal flags. From the bridge of his boat *Catherine*, the king himself, Charles II, looks over the newly built yacht *Anne*, where his brother James, Duke of York, is on board. A man of rude health and with a sporting disposition, the king had discovered sailing during the years he spent in exile in Holland. There, it was easier to move around on water than to traverse the few existing roads. While in Holland Charles II had also fortuitously received the gift of a yacht from a Dutch nobleman, and this emboldened him the following year to commission *Catherine* to be built by Christopher Pett, the renowned master axe maker. Not to be outdone, the Duke of York immediately ordered Peter Pett, Christopher's brother, to construct *Anne*. As the two yachts challenged each other on a 40 mile stretch along the Thames from Greenwich to Gravesend and back (for a purse of 100 pounds sterling), the sailing regatta was born.

Prior to 1661 sailing challenges were largely the preserve of commercial yachts. The clippers, famously, transported tea and wool across the globe, and those goods which were first to arrive in port not only often doubled in value, but the captain responsible was presented with a golden weathercock to be displayed with pride. In this regard, the sport of sailing had a distinctly mercantile origin. With the founding of the Cumberland Fleet – precursor of the current Royal Thames Yacht Club – in the mid eighteenth century, the notion of the regatta was developed further, but it was not really until the Royal Yacht Squadron organised the first series of day races at Cowes in 1826 that the regatta first found its feet. This annual August week long event is now by common consent thought to be the world's oldest regular regatta.

Today, increasingly, many regatta dates are not only overloaded but conflicting. The competing needs of class, yacht club, sponsor, crew and owner are being juggled like never before. As a result, the regattas which have withstood the test of time are few: the Sydney-Hobart, Antigua Sailing Week, the SORC in Florida and the Volvo Ocean Race being among the more well known.

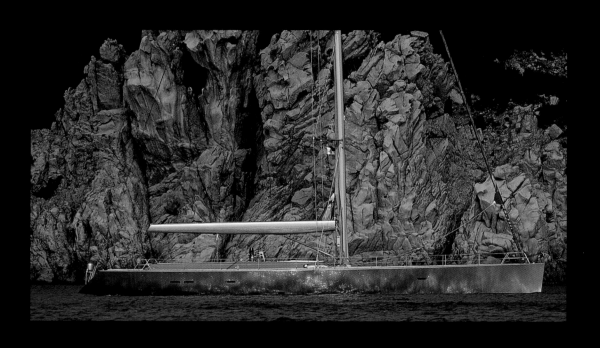

On board the G Class *Club Med*, one of the giant multihulls that, with a length in excess of 98ft (30m), dominate the great ocean races. (C Borlenghi)

The 470 Olympic class racing dinghy is shown here during the 2004 Olympic trials and Hyeres in France. (H Thibault)

The Soling World Championships, held at Grosseto, May 2005. (R J Taylor)

A Soling competes in Hyeres, France. (C Borlenghi)

A 49-er Class during the 2004 Olympics in Athens. (C Borlenghi)

Italy's Lake Garda is an ideal arena for small craft racing events. (C Borlenghi)

A Laser during an event at Lake Garda, 2004. (C Borlenghi)

Francesco De Angelis and Torben Grael skipper and tactician, respectively, of *Luna Rossa*. (C Borlenghi)

Luna Rossa continues to be the strongest Italian America's Cup syndicate. (P Todd)

The trimaran *Tim* is owned by Giovanni Soldini and is a permanent fixture at the Three Gulfs Regatta, held each year in the waters around Naples, Salerno and Gaeta. (C Borlenghi)

Tim is the result of the collaborative design work of the French firm Van Peteghem-Lauriot Prevost.

Bonduelle appears to take off in this image, taken in the waters of Cap d'Agde, France. (C Borlenghi)

The catamaran *Club Med* at the starting line of the 2000 around the world event The Race. (C Borlenghi)

Foncia is an extremely fast trimaran measuring 60ft (18m). (G M Raget)

Despite its launch close to 10 years ago, *Groupama* is still competitive. (G M Raget)

Experienced sailor Florence Arthaud on board *Pierre 1ere*. Right: the impressive acrobatics of *Belgacom*. (G M Raget)

The Van Peteghem-Lauriot Prevost designed *Sodebo*. (G M Raget)

Belgacom was built with the open ocean in mind. (G M Raget)

'Circling', left, is a standard pre start tactic that limits an adversary's manoeuvrability. (C Borlenghi)

Alinghi won the 2003 America's Cup with surprising ease and continues to dominate events held in the run-up to Valencia in 2007.

One of the fundamental rules of yacht racing stipulates that it is always best to place oneself between buoy and opponent. Here, however, the trailing yacht has a distinct advantage.

Left, *Alinghi* rounds a buoy to starboard. (C Borlenghi)

The start of the 1995 America's Cup in San Diego. Ninety percent of any race's outcome is established by the time a competitor reaches the first mark. (C Borlenghi)

By hanging from a mast's highest crosstree the capriciousness of the wind is more easily gauged. (C Borlenghi)

Banque Populaire is only the third 60ft (18m) trimaran to be built. Skippered by Lalou Roucayrol and designed by Marc Lombard it is photographed here at the Grand Prix de Fécamp. (C Borlenghi)

Multihulls

'WE HAVE DISCOVERED A NEW AND BETTER SYSTEM OF SAILING' WROTE THE ENGLISH INVENTOR, PHYSICIST AND ANATOMIST WILLIAM PETTY IN 1662. KING CHARLES II, A FIRST-RATE SAILOR HIMSELF, CALLED IT A 'FANTASTIC DOUBLE-HULLED MACHINE'. ARISING OUT OF PETTY'S HYPOTHESIS THAT IF A NARROW AND SHARP HULL IS ABLE TO CLEAVE THE WAVES LIKE AN ARROW, THEN TWO EQUAL-SIZED HULLS WHICH ARE JOINED TOGETHER BY A BRIDGE OUGHT TO OFFER SIMILAR SPEED WITHOUT THE THREAT OF CAPSIZE, HE NAMED IT *INVENTION* AND IMMEDIATELY SET ABOUT BUILDING TWO MORE. *EXPERIMENT* DREW LESS THAN 2FT (1/2M) AND SANK IN A STORM INTENDED TO DEMONSTRATE ITS SAFETY; *ST MICHAEL* WAS SCRAPPED DUE TO INSTABILITY.

IT TOOK ANOTHER TWO CENTURIES BEFORE FURTHER SIGNIFICANT EXPERIMENTS ON MULTIHULLS TOOK PLACE. IN 1875, NAT HERRESHOFF, ARGUABLY THE MOST IMPORTANT AMERICAN BOAT DESIGNER OF ALL TIME, WROTE THAT: 'A SAIL BOAT WITH TWO HULLS, HELD TOGETHER BY THREE BEAMS, THE INTERMEDIATE ONE SUPPORTING THE MASTER ... FAST BOATS THAT CAN DO 20 KNOTS ABEAM ... THEY ARE THE ONES WHICH DELIGHT ME MOST'. IN THE END, HERRESHOFF CONTINUED TO DELIGHT HIMSELF BY DESIGNING NUMEROUS PRESTIGIOUS BIG BOATS, BUT DEVELOPED ONLY A LIMITED NUMBER OF CATAMARAN MODELS AT 20FT, 25FT AND 32 FT (6M, 8M AND 10M)

THE MULTIHULL PHENOMENON BEGAN TO COME TO FRUITION BY THE 1970S. AT THE OSTAR SINGLE-HANDED TRANSATLANTIC RACE OF 1964 THERE WERE THREE MULTIHULLS IN COMPETITION. FOUR YEARS LATER THERE WERE 13, AND THEIR PRESENCE THEREAFTER CONTINUED TO GROW EXPONENTIALLY UNTIL THEY WOUND UP DOMINATING, AS THEY DO TODAY, ALL OF THE GREAT OCEAN RACES.

BY THE END OF THE 1980S A SINGLE, STANDARD MAXIMUM LENGTH OF 60FT (18M) WAS SPECIFIED FOR ALL OCEAN-COMPETING MULTIHULLS. THIS SIZE WAS DEEMED TO BE IDEAL FOR SAILING EITHER ALONE OR WITH A CREW. TELLINGLY, THIS LENGTH REMAINED CONSTANT EVEN AS SUBSEQUENT GENERATIONS OF DESIGNERS WROUGHT SUBSTANTIAL CHANGES IN THE FORM OF CONSTRUCTION MATERIALS (CARBON), MASTS (OSCILLATING) AND HULLS (BEARING WINGS). HOWEVER, WITH THE INTRODUCTION OF THE NON-STOP RACE AROUND THE WORLD, THE RACE, WHERE ANY KIND OF VESSEL COULD BE EMPLOYED AS LONG AS IT WAS PROPELLED EXCLUSIVELY BY THE WIND, SIZES BECAME LARGER. CATAMARANS SUDDENLY GREW TO IN EXCESS OF 98FT (30M) AND WERE CAPABLE OF TRAVELLING MORE THAN 500 MILES (800KM) PER DAY, WITH AN AVERAGE SPEED OF OVER 20 KNOTS. THE FUTURE OF SAILING HAD ALREADY ARRIVED.

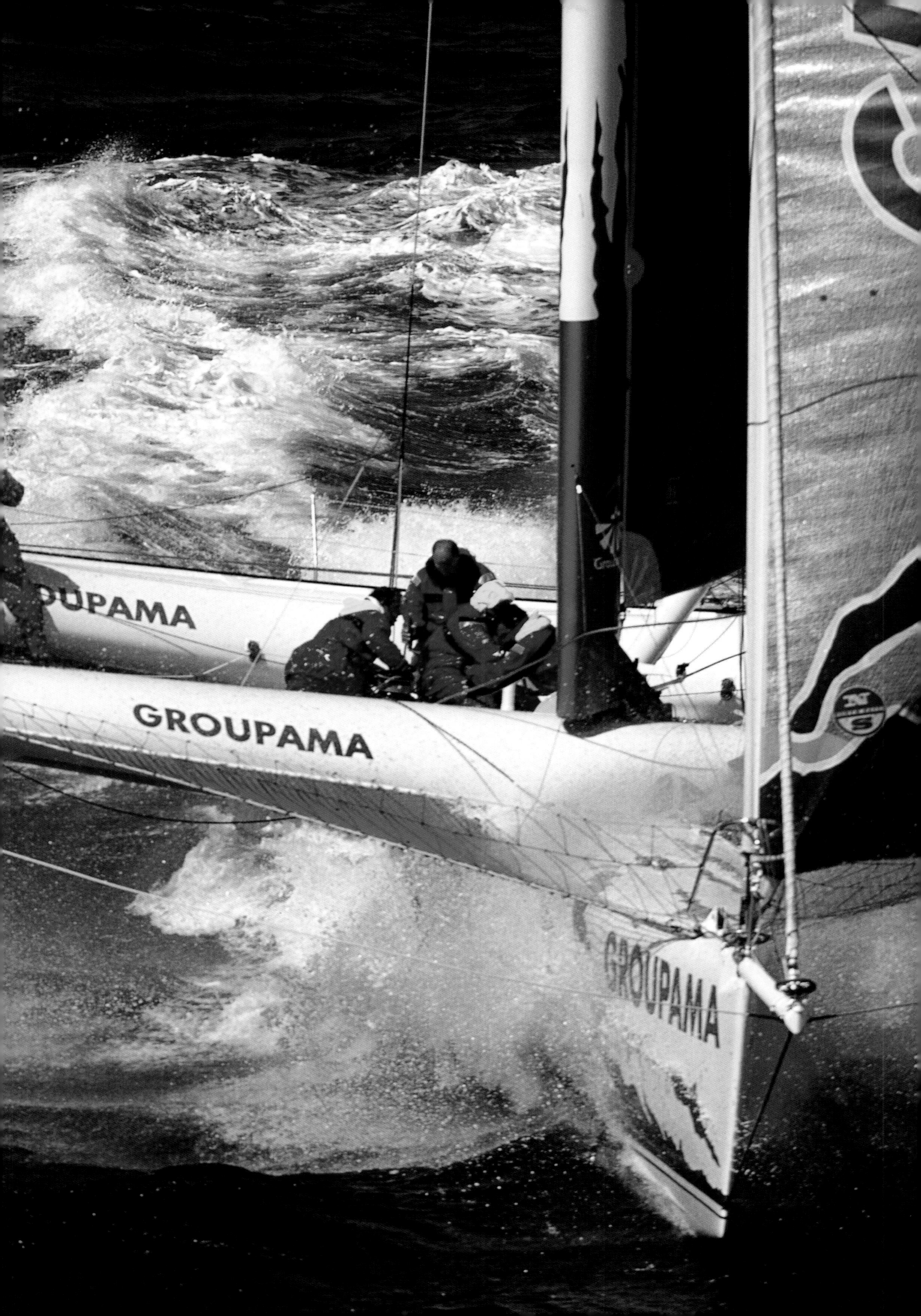
OUPAMA
GROUPAMA
GROUPAMA

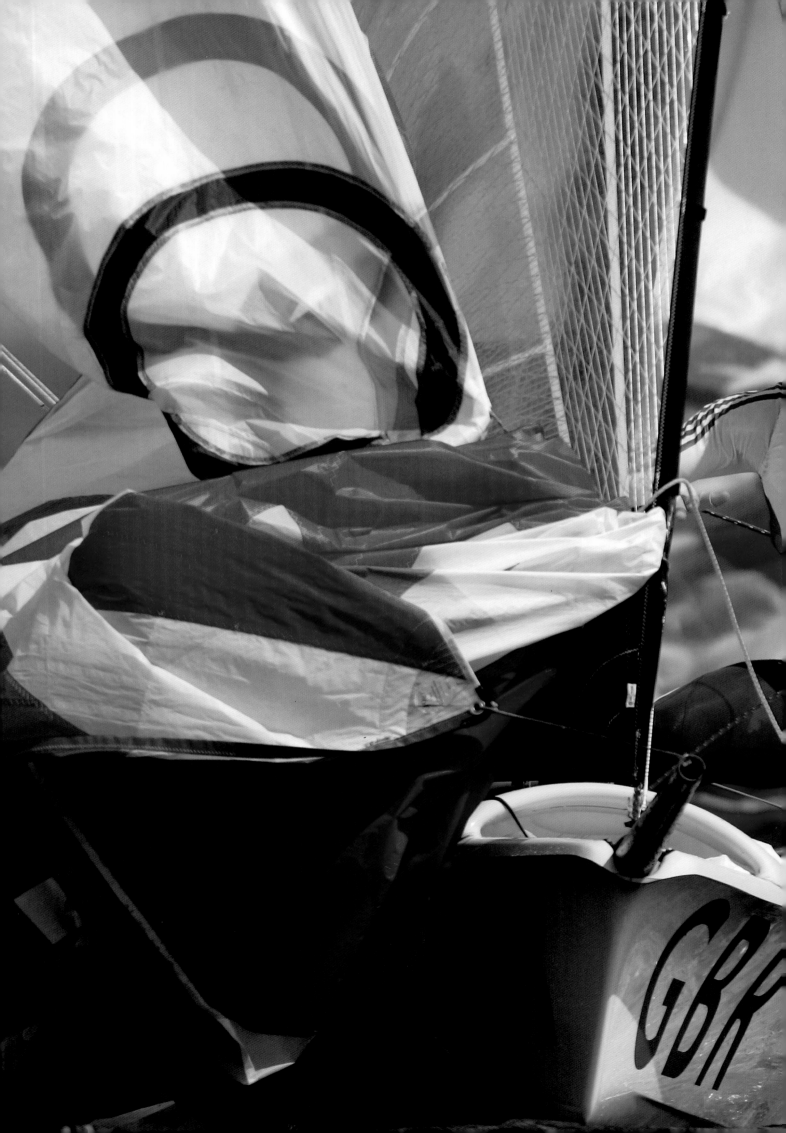

AMERICA'S CUP

THE SCHOONER *AMERICA*, DESIGNED BY THE YOUNG NEW YORKER GEORGE STEERS IN 1851, HAD A HULL MEASURING SLIGHTLY MORE THAN 98FT (30M), A BRIDGE FREE OF ANY OTHER STRUCTURE AND A COCKPIT STERN WELL FOR THE HELMSMAN THAT WAS SURROUNDED BY CIRCULAR COAMING. AS LEGEND WOULD HAVE IT, *AMERICA* CROSSED THE OCEAN, ANCHORED IN FRONT OF THE ROYAL YACHT SQUADRON IN COWES, TOSSED HER GLOVE SIGNALLING A CHALLENGE TO DUEL, AND PROMPTLY SET ABOUT BEATING AN ENTIRE FLEET OF ADVERSARIES IN A 53 MILE REGATTA (IN BOTH REAL AND ADJUSTED TIME). THE AMERICA'S CUP, IT SEEMS, HAD ARRIVED IN STYLE.

NEVERTHELESS, AFTER HER TRIUMPH, *AMERICA* WAS TO REMAIN IN EUROPE WITH DIFFERENT OWNERS FOR CLOSED TO 10 YEARS. AND WHEN HER CAREER CAME TO AN OFFICIAL CLOSE AT THE HANDS OF GENERAL BENJAMIN BUTLER IN 1901 — BUTLER HAD USED HER FOR RECREATIONAL PURPOSES — SHE ENDED HER DAYS IN A RATHER CURIOUS WAY FOR A YACHT: WHILE UNDER A SHED UNDER-GOING REPAIR IN 1942 SHE WAS TURNED UPSIDE DOWN WHEN THE ROOF CAVED-IN DURING AN EXCEPTIONALLY VIOLENT SNOWSTORM. NINETY-TWO YEARS HAD PASSED SINCE HER LAUNCH.

THE AMERICA'S CUP HAS HISTORICALLY SUFFERED PROBLEMS RESULTING FROM A LACK OF A COMMON SPECIFICATION STANDARD. THOMAS LIPTON CHANGED THIS WHEN HE CONVINCED THE US TO ACCEPT THE J CLASS UNIVERSAL RULE STANDARD IN 1913, AND IN 1958 THE 12 METRE INTERNATIONAL CLASS WAS BORN, MEASURING ALMOST HALF THE LENGTH OF THE J CLASS. WHEN THE DESIGNER BEN LEXCEN LITERALLY PUT WINGS ON THE KEEL OF *AUSTRALIA II* IN 1983, THE LONGEST WINNING STREAK IN THE HISTORY OF SPORT CAME TO AN END. (THE AMERICA'S CUP TROPHY REMAINED IN US HANDS FROM 1851 TO 1983.)

UNFORTUNATELY, DARK DAYS FOLLOWED IN THE FORM OF SEVERAL YEARS OF HIGHLY SUSPECT INTERPRETATIONS OF THE UNIVERSAL RULE, WITH EVENTS REACHING THEIR NADIR IN 1988 WHEN A 129FT (39M) MONOHULL FROM NEW ZEALAND WAS PUT IN COMPETITION AGAINST A 63FT (19M) CATAMARAN FROM THE US. FINALLY, IN THE 1990S THE AMERICA'S CUP ADOPTED THE IACC (INTERNATIONAL AMERICA'S CUP CLASS). THE IACC STIPULATES A LENGTH OF 87FT (27M), A WEIGHT OF 25 TONS, A SAILING BOWLINE SURFACE OF 3,983 SQ FT (370M), A STERN OF 7,859 SQ FT (730 SQ M) AND A KEEL 14 FT (4M) DEEP WITH A LEAD BULB ONTO WHICH WINGS ARE ATTACHED.

TODAY'S CHALLENGERS CROSS OCEANS, TOO, OF COURSE, JUST AS THEIR PREDECESSORS DID, ONLY THEY DO IT ON BOARD A CARGO SHIP OR IN THE BELLY OF AN AEROPLANE. THEIR LIFESPANS ARE SHORTER AS WELL — LASTING, IN MANY CASES, ONLY AS LONG AS THE RACE FOR WHICH THEY WERE BUILT. WIN OR LOSE, THEIR FATE IS NOT TO RUN THE RACE AGAIN.

Opposite page: *New Zealand* (D Forster). On the previous pages: *Luna Rossa* (C Borlenghi)